THE

INEVITABLE

APPOINTMENT

Rev. Dr. William Wood

<u>Foreword</u>

Rev. Dr. William Wood's ministry is widely respected in the UK and abroad, he has been anointed to write this book in a time of change and uncertainty in our world.

We are I believe, truly living in a time when "men's hearts are failing them from fear and the expectation of things which are coming on the earth" as Jesus says in Luke 21 v. 26.

 Rev. Wood awakens the reader to the reality of the fragility of life, but treats the subject with skill and sensitivity. He brings a new depth of revelation from the Bible, on what for many is a taboo subject.

This book is about life because Rev. Wood ultimately **focuses** on how we should live our lives here on earth considering that we will all face the "inevitable appointment."

This book will appeal to you whether you are a mature Christian or an honest seeker after truth. It will be a means of bringing hope, reassurance and of deepening your daily walk with the Lord.

I thoroughly recommend it.

Minister Bob & Dorothy Cromwell

January 2007

Wood World Missions Publications

Wood World Missions

118-120 London Road

Mitcham

Surrey,

CR4 3LB

ISBN-13: 978-1999919535

NKJV – Authorised version of the Bible. Crown copyright

Printed in England

CONTENTS

INTRODUCTION

One thing I have noticed over the years is that when a woman is pregnant she makes sure everyone knows about it. She also prepares for the coming of the child. When the child is born, everyone who needs to know is told of the child's birth. The birth is followed by a time of celebration. However, when it comes to death, people are very reluctant to raise the subject let alone discuss it.

When I told one or two people about my intention of writing a book about death, the expression on their face was enough to dissuade me from putting pen to paper. However, after much prayer and research, I knew it was right for me to bring this book into the public domain.

It is my sincere belief that since death will come to us all one day, it is of great importance that we know something about it, and be properly prepared for it.

As you read this book, it is my prayer that it will enlighten you and enable you to be better prepared to meet death when it comes.

May the Lord guide you through your reading of this book and lead you to make the right choices in this life so that all he has in store for you in Christ can become a reality in the fullness of time.

I am not only truly grateful to God for enabling me to write this book, but to Rev. Ingrid Friday-Young, Minister Dorothy Cromwell and Mr. Bob

Cromwell for taking the time to read through this book prior to its publication.
Stay Blessed in Jesus name.

Rev. Dr. William Wood
LLB (Hons) BL; Dip.MT; DM
©2007

Chapter 1

The Inevitable Alternatives

One second after we die we will either be enjoying a personal welcome from Christ or catching our first glimpse of gloom as we have never known it before. After death, there will be many regrets for those who did not walk according to the promptings of the Word of God. Our memories and feelings will be fully intact and there will be an indescribable weight of guilt for some and abandonment for others. Those who did not give their lives to Jesus will soon realise that the eulogy and beautiful words spoken about them at their funeral service bear no resemblance to the reality confronting them after death.

As you read this book it is my prayer that you will realise quite quickly that whilst we are alive, we must begin to live a life of sacrifice for Christ. It is also my sincere hope that in reading this book you will come to the conclusion that the best investments are those that are safe and permanent. If you are wise, you will spend your time preparing for that, which lasts forever.

Death is not only inevitable, but it is much nearer than we think. Just as a wise traveller first obtains maps and guidebooks before they travel, it is my submission that as Christians we must get our maps and guidebooks that will lead us into the presence of God. I suggest that the maps and guidebooks that we need are the Word of God, Jesus, the Holy Spirit and God. If we have all of these in our lives today and we move daily in accordance with the dictates of those guides, we will end up receiving a personal welcome from Christ after our death.

We also need to know that just as Heaven is inviting, Hell is fearsome. Where we end up after death will depend on the choices we make today. We will all face death individually and we need to properly prepare for death as individuals. Some people have had near death experiences and others have been revived from the dead. The bottom line however, is that we will all die one day and the onus is on us to properly prepare for our death so that when it comes, we are not taken by surprise. We need to ensure that we do not end up on the wrong side of eternity.

Chapter 2

The History of Death

Death as we know it today came to humanity as a consequence of Adam and Eve's disobedience in the Garden of Eden. As soon as Adam and Eve sinned against God, they died spiritually. It was instant and separated them from God. It was at this point that physical death was introduced into the world.

God did not want Adam and Eve to eat of the tree of life and live forever in their sins, he drove them out of the Garden of Eden so that in the fullness of time his son Jesus could come and be the source through which human kind would be reconciled back to God. By driving them away from the Garden of Eden, God saved man in his sinful state.

THE OLD TESTAMENT

The most important word in the Old Testament that speaks of the afterlife is the Hebrew word "Sheol". The word Sheol appears 65 times in the Old Testament. In the King James Version of the Bible, it is translated hell 31 times, grave 31 times and pit 3 times. This inconsistency in the translation has caused some to be confused as to what Sheol really means. Sheol is clearly distinguished from hell. Sheol does not refer only to the grave. The writers of the Old Testament believed that to go to Sheol was not only to go to the grave but also to experience a conscious afterlife.

<u>WHAT THE OLD TESTAMENT MEANS BY THE WORD SHEOL</u>

1. There is a clear distinction between the grave where the body rests and Sheol where the spirits of the dead gather. (Isaiah 14:9-10). Sheol is not a neutral place. It is a place of activity.
2. Sheol is often spoken of as a shadowy place of darkness. A place that is not part of this existence. (Ezekiel 26:20 & Job. 26:5-6).
3. After death, one can be united with ones ancestors in Sheol. (Genesis 49:33 & Genesis 15:15).

4. There are hints in the Old Testament that Sheol has different regions. Both the wicked and the righteous are said to go to Sheol.

According to the scriptures, Jacob went to Sheol and so did rebellious people such as Korah and Dathan. Whereas Jacob would have gone to the upper region of Sheol, people like Korah and Dothan would have gone to the lower region of Sheol. (Deuteronomy 32:22).

If you read the following scriptures they will tell you that Sheol has two different kinds of inhabitants – the wicked and the righteous – (Psalm 49:13-15; Job 24:19; Psalm 9:17; Psalm 16:9-10; Psalm 31:17 & Psalm 55:15). In addition to these scriptures, Daniel 12:2 also makes reference to the New

Testament doctrine of the resurrection of the body.

In summary therefore, Sheol according to Old Testament belief was a region of departed spirits – the wicked and the righteous.

WHAT THE NEW TESTAMENT MEANS BY THE WORD SHEOL

The New Testament was written in Greek. The Greek word for Sheol is Hades. Like Sheol, Hades is always used to refer to the world of departed spirits.

If we read the story of the rich man and Lazarus as recorded in the book of Luke 16:19-31the Bible tells us that when the rich man died, his soul was taken to Hades. The story also tells us that when Lazarus died, he was carried into Abraham's bosom – the blissful region of Hades.

It is important for us to note that our riches or lack of them do not dictate our eternal destiny. The rich man's riches could not save him from going to the terrible section of Hades. The rich man ended up in the place of acute distress.

<u>Chapter 3</u>

<u>Lessons from Luke 16:19-31 – the rich man and Lazarus</u>

<u>Luke 16:19-31</u>

The Rich Man and Lazarus

19 "There was a certain rich man who was clothed in purple and fine linen and fared sumptuously every day. 20 But there was a certain beggar named Lazarus, full of sores, who was laid at his gate, 21 desiring to be fed with the crumbs, which fell from the rich man's table. Moreover the dogs came and licked his sores. 22 So it was that the beggar died, and was carried by the

angels to Abraham's bosom. The rich man also died and was buried. 23 And being in torments in Hades, he lifted up his eyes and saw Abraham afar off, and Lazarus in his bosom. 24 "Then he cried and said, 'Father Abraham, have mercy on me, and send Lazarus that he may dip the tip of his finger in water and cool my tongue; for I am tormented in this flame.' 25 But Abraham said, 'Son, remember that in your lifetime you received your good things, and likewise Lazarus evil things; but now he is comforted and you are tormented. 26 And besides all this, between us and you there is a great gulf fixed, so that those who want to pass from here to you cannot, nor can those from there pass to us.' 27 "Then he said, 'I beg you therefore, father, that you would send him to my father's house, 28 for I have five brothers, that he may testify to them, lest they also come to this place of torment.' 29 Abraham said to him, 'They have Moses and the prophets; let them hear them.' 30 And he said, 'No, father Abraham; but if one goes to them from the dead, they will repent.' 31 But he said to him, 'If they do not hear Moses and the prophets, neither will they be persuaded though one rise from the dead.'"

1. The rich man in Hades was fully conscious immediately after death.
2. He had his memory intact.
3. He could speak.
4. He could feel pain. Lazarus on the other hand could experience the bliss – Luke 16:24.
5. In Hades, the rich man was experiencing increased desire with

decreased satisfaction – Proverbs 27:20.

6. In Hades, the eternal destinies of both the rich man and Lazarus had become irrevocably fixed – Luke 16:26.

7. The rich man, whilst in Hades knew that what he was experiencing was fair and just – (Luke 16:28). If you examine closely the words used by the rich man, at no point did he raise the issue of why he was in the terrible region of Hades. He knew in his heart of hearts that he was in the right place and that God was right in placing him there. This tells me that anyone who finds themselves in the rich man's situation will know that God was right in placing them there. If there are any changes we can make, I

suggest the time to make them is now.

8. One notes from the scriptures that the rich man incredibly suddenly became interested in missions. It was however too late for him to do anything about this newly developed interest. He should have engaged himself in mission work whilst he was alive and well here on earth.

9. Whilst in Hades, the rich man realised that his relationship with God should have been his highest priority whilst he was alive. Now, it was too late for him.

10. Even though today the evidence of Jesus' resurrection is so overwhelming, many people still do not believe in Jesus Christ as the risen Saviour and Lord.

11. It is worth noting that at this point the rich man was not yet in hell but in Hades. (Revelation 20:14).

12. The Bible is very clear about the fact that no one is yet in hell today. Someday in the future, Hades will be thrown into hell. That has not taken place yet. (Revelation 20:14 & 2 Peter 2:9).

13. Lazarus on the other hand was in the blissful part of Hades. He was in Abraham's bosom.

14. The Bible is also clear about the fact that after the ascension of Jesus Christ, Christians are said to go directly into Heaven when they die. The Bible says in 2 Corinthians 5:8 that "… to be absent from the body is to be present with the Lord…"

15. As at today, the two regions of Hades no longer exist side by side. Abraham's bosom is in Heaven. Hades as far as we know now has only one region and no Christians go there when they die.

One second after we die we will be either elated or terrified. Which of these will it be for you? The choice is yours. Jesus put it this way "…I have placed before you life and death. Choose life and live…"

Chapter 4

The benefits of death for a Christian

Anyone who dies as a Christian will experience a number of benefits. The benefits are as follows:

1. Only death can give us the gift of eternity. Not until one dies, can one enjoy the gift of spending eternity with God in Heaven. Death therefore is the gateway into eternity. One has to die in order to go to Heaven.
2. Death releases us into the presence of God.

3. Death introduces us to riches eternal. The riches we will be faced with in Heaven cannot be compared with the riches we enjoy here on earth.

4. Death gives us the right to the tree of life. This is the tree that Adam and Eve were prevented from eating in the Garden of Eden.

5. Death might temporarily take us away from our friends but only to introduce us to that land in which there are no goodbyes.

6. Death preserves our soul, mind, emotions and will. (Matthew 10:28). When the executioners have done their worst, God will be shown to have done His best for us.

7. Death is the means by which our bodies are put to rest while our spirits are escorted through the

gates of Heaven. In effect, death brings us to the gate and Jesus opens the door to the gate for us. (Revelation 3:7 & Hebrews 2:14-15).

8. Death is the means by which those who love God are finally brought to him.

9. Only on this side of the curtain is death our enemy. Just beyond the curtain, death, the monster turns out to be our friend.

10. Death should remind us of how near Heaven is to us. Heaven is as near as a heartbeat, an accident, a stray bullet, a heart attack, a plane crash a bomb explosion or our next breath.

11. Death is not the end of our Christian road. It is only a bend in the road. We will only meet Christ in Heaven if we have met him here on

earth (John 14:3). Heaven is a special place for special people. We must aim to be special people to God here on earth in order to have the privilege of spending eternity with him in Heaven.

Chapter 5

Five descriptions of death in the New Testament

In the New Testament, five figures of speech are used to describe death. It is transformed from being a monster to a minister. Death has been described in the New Testament as follows:

1. **DEPARTURE:** – Departure in Greek is Exodus. It is from this word that we get the word exit. (Exodus 9:1). Just as Moses, the qualified leader led the children of Israel out of Egypt into the Promised Land, Jesus, our even more qualified leader will lead us out of this earth into our promised land. (John 13:36).

2. **<u>A RESTFUL SLEEP</u>**: If you read the following scriptures, you will find death referred to as a restful sleep. (Luke 8:52, John 11:11 & 1 Corinthians 15:51). After all the hustle and bustle on this earth, sleep will be a welcome experience for those who need not fear the morning. Revelation 14:13.

3. **<u>A COLLAPSING TENT</u>**: in 2 Corinthians 5:1, Paul describes death as a collapsing tent. A tent reminds us that we are only pilgrims here on earth en route to our final home. If we walk closely with the Lord, death will in the end change our address from earth to Heaven.

4. **<u>A SAILING SHIP</u>**: If you read Philippians 1:23-24; 2 Timothy 4:6 & Hebrews 6:19-20, death is

referred to as a sailing ship. We are pilgrims on this earth on our way to an eternal destination. Which of the two destinations will it be for you? The choice is yours.

5. **THE WAY TO OUR PERMANENT HOME**: In John 14:2-3 and 2 Corinthians 5:6-8, death is seen as the instrument by which we are brought to our permanent home. In 1 Corinthians 15:55 the Bible says "oh death where is thy sting?"

Two thousand years ago, the truck of death run over the Lord Jesus Christ. Today only the shadow of death can run over us. That is why the Bible says in Psalm 23:4 that "…yea though I walk through the valley of the shadow of death, I shall fear no evil, for thou art with me…" Death is the chariot that our Heavenly Father sends to bring us to himself.

As Christians, when the time comes for us to die, we ought to be ready. We can be ready if we properly prepare for that final second. We must be able to say like Jesus said, "…it is finished…" When we die, our loved ones will bury our body but they cannot bury the real us which is our spirit. We must be able to say at the point of our death what Jesus said,

"… Father into thy hands I commit my spirit…it is finished…"

Chapter 6

What we should expect in Heaven

There are a number of things we can expect when we get to Heaven. The scriptures teach us to expect the following when we get to Heaven:

1. In Heaven, our personal knowledge will continue. Our minds and our memories will be clearer than ever before. If we look closely at the story of the rich man and Lazarus as recounted in Luke 16:19-31, it is quite clear that both the rich man and Lazarus had good memories even after death. (1 Corinthians 13:12).
2. In Heaven the desire to sin will no longer be a part of our being. We

need to begin to cultivate that habit here on earth. We must begin to live on earth with Heaven in mind. (Romans 8:18). We must begin to practice living in Heaven here on earth.

3. In Heaven, our personal feelings will continue. Our mind and our emotions will be intact. (Psalm 16:11; Revelation 7:17; Revelation 21:4 & Revelation 6:9-10). In the story of the rich man and Lazarus, it is stated clearly that the rich man could feel the pain generated by his immediate surroundings after his death.

4. In Heaven, personal activities will continue. Even though we will rest whilst in Heaven, our rest will not be a rest of inactivity. We will be worshiping God and carrying out

other such pleasant activities. (Revelation 19:5-6).

5. In Heaven we will be serving God. (Revelation 22:3-4; Matthew 4:10; Luke 2:37 & Acts 24:14).

6. Everyone in Heaven will be joyful and fulfilled unlike those who will find themselves in the lower region of Hades and ultimately in Hell. (Revelation 20:14 and 2 Peter 2:9).

Chapter 7

Things that will be absent in Heaven

<u>Revelation 7</u>

The Sealed of Israel

1 After these things I saw four angels standing at the four corners of the earth, holding the four winds of the earth, that the wind should not blow on the earth, on the sea, or on any tree. 2 Then I saw another angel ascending from the east, having the seal of the living God. And he cried with a loud voice to the four angels to whom it was granted to harm the earth and the sea, 3 saying, "Do not harm the earth, the sea, or the trees till we have sealed the servants of our God on their

foreheads." 4 And I heard the number of those who were sealed. One hundred *and* forty-four thousand of all the tribes of the children of Israel *were* sealed:

5 of the tribe of Judah twelve thousand *were* sealed;

of the tribe of Reuben twelve thousand *were* sealed;

of the tribe of Gad twelve thousand *were* sealed;

6 of the tribe of Asher twelve thousand *were* sealed;

of the tribe of Naphtali twelve thousand *were* sealed;

of the tribe of Manasseh twelve thousand *were* sealed;

7 of the tribe of Simeon twelve thousand *were* sealed;

of the tribe of Levi twelve thousand *were* sealed;

of the tribe of Issachar twelve

thousand *were* sealed;

8 of the tribe of Zebulun twelve thousand *were* sealed; of the tribe of Joseph twelve thousand *were* sealed; of the tribe of Benjamin twelve thousand *were* sealed.

A Multitude from the Great Tribulation

9 After these things I looked, and behold, a great multitude which no one could number, of all nations, tribes, peoples, and tongues, standing before the throne and before the Lamb, clothed with white robes, with palm branches in their hands, 10 and crying out with a loud voice, saying, "Salvation *belongs* to our God who sits on the throne, and to the Lamb!" 11

All the angels stood around the throne and the elders and the four living creatures, and fell on their faces before the throne and worshiped God, 12 saying:

"Amen! Blessing and glory and wisdom,

Thanksgiving and honour and power and might,

Be to our God forever and ever. Amen."

13 Then one of the elders answered, saying to me, "Who are these arrayed in white robes, and where did they come from?"

14 And I said to him, "Sir, you know." So he said to me, "These are the ones who come out of the great tribulation, and washed their robes and made them white in the blood of the Lamb. 15 Therefore they are before the throne of God, and serve Him day and night in

His temple. And He who sits on the throne will dwell among them. 16 They shall neither hunger anymore nor thirst anymore; the sun shall not strike them, nor any heat; 17 for the Lamb who is in the midst of the throne will shepherd them and lead them to living fountains of waters. And God will wipe away every tear from their eyes."

<u>Revelation 21</u>

All Things Made New

1 Now I saw a new heaven and a new earth, for the first heaven and the first earth had passed away. Also there was no more sea. 2 Then I, John, saw the holy city, New Jerusalem, coming down out of heaven from God, prepared as a bride adorned for her husband. 3 And I heard a loud voice from heaven saying, "Behold, the

tabernacle of God *is* with men, and He will dwell with them, and they shall be His people. God Himself will be with them *and be* their God. 4 And God will wipe away every tear from their eyes; there shall be no more death, nor sorrow, nor crying. There shall be no more pain, for the former things have passed   away."

5 Then He who sat on the throne said, "Behold, I make all things new." And He said to me, "Write, for these words are   true   and   faithful."

6 And He said to me, "It is done! I am the Alpha and the Omega, the Beginning and the End. I will give of the fountain of the water of life freely to   him   who   thirsts. 7 He who overcomes shall inherit all things, and I will be his God and he shall be My son. 8 But the cowardly, unbelieving, abominable,   murderers,   sexually

immoral, sorcerers, idolaters, and all liars shall have their part in the lake which burns with fire and brimstone, which is the second death."

The New Jerusalem

9 Then one of the seven angels who had the seven bowls filled with the seven last plagues came to me and talked with me, saying, "Come, I will show you the bride, the Lamb's wife." 10 And he carried me away in the Spirit to a great and high mountain, and showed me the great city, the holy Jerusalem, descending out of heaven from God, 11 having the glory of God. Her light *was* like a most precious stone, like a jasper stone, clear as crystal. 12 Also she had a great and high wall with twelve gates, and twelve angels at the gates, and names written

on them, which are *the names* of the
twelve tribes of the children of Israel:
13 three gates on the east, three gates
on the north, three gates on the south,
and three gates on the west.
14 Now the wall of the city had twelve
foundations, and on them were the
names of the twelve apostles of the
Lamb. 15 And he who talked with me
had a gold reed to measure the city, its
gates, and its wall. 16 The city is laid
out as a square; its length is as great as
its breadth. And he measured the city
with the reed: twelve thousand
furlongs. Its length, breadth, and
height are equal. 17 Then he measured
its wall: one hundred *and* forty-four
cubits, *according* to the measure of a
man, that is, of an angel. 18 The
construction of its wall was *of* jasper;
and the city *was* pure gold, like clear
glass. 19 The foundations of the wall

of the city *were* adorned with all kinds of precious stones: the first foundation *was* jasper, the second sapphire, the third chalcedony, the fourth emerald, 20 the fifth sardonyx, the sixth sardius, the seventh chrysolite, the eighth beryl, the ninth topaz, the tenth chrysoprase, the eleventh jacinth, and the twelfth amethyst. 21 The twelve gates *were* twelve pearls: each individual gate was of one pearl. And the street of the city *was* pure gold, like transparent glass.

The Glory of the New Jerusalem

22 But I saw no temple in it, for the Lord God Almighty and the Lamb are its temple. 23 The city had no need of the sun or of the moon to shine in it, for the glory of God illuminated it. The Lamb *is* its light. 24 And the nations of those who are saved shall walk in its

light, and the kings of the earth bring their glory and honor into it.25 Its gates shall not be shut at all by day (there shall be no night there). 26 And they shall bring the glory and the honor of the nations into it. 27 But there shall by no means enter it anything that defiles, or causes an abomination or a lie, but only those who are written in the Lamb's Book of Life.

<u>Revelation 22</u>

The River of Life

1 And he showed me a pure river of water of life, clear as crystal, proceeding from the throne of God and of the Lamb. 2 In the middle of its street, and on either side of the river,

was the tree of life, which bore twelve fruits, each *tree* yielding its fruit every month. The leaves of the tree *were* for the healing of the nations. 3 And there shall be no more curse, but the throne of God and of the Lamb shall be in it, and His servants shall serve Him. 4 They shall see His face, and His name *shall be* on their foreheads. 5 There shall be no night there: They need no lamp nor light of the sun, for the Lord God gives them light. And they shall reign forever and ever.

The Time Is Near

6 Then he said to me, "These words *are* faithful and true." And the Lord God of the holy prophets sent His angel to show His servants the things, which must shortly take place. 7 "Behold, I am coming quickly!

Blessed *is* he who keeps the words of the prophecy of this book." 8 Now I, John, saw and heard these things. And when I heard and saw, I fell down to worship before the feet of the angel who showed me these things. 9 Then he said to me, "See *that you do* not *do that*. For I am your fellow servant, and of your brethren the prophets, and of those who keep the words of this book. Worship God." 10 And he said to me, "Do not seal the words of the prophecy of this book, for the time is at hand. 11 He who is unjust, let him be unjust still; he who is filthy, let him be filthy still; he who is righteous, let him be righteous still; he who is holy, let him be holy still."

Jesus Testifies to the Churches

12 "And behold, I am coming quickly,

and My reward *is* with Me, to give to every one according to his work. 13 I am the Alpha and the Omega, *the* Beginning and *the* End, the First and the   Last."
14 Blessed *are* those who do His commandments, that they may have the right to the tree of life, and may enter through the gates into the city. 15 But outside *are* dogs and sorcerers and sexually immoral and murderers and idolaters, and whoever loves and practices   a   lie.
16 "I, Jesus, have sent My angel to testify to you these things in the churches. I am the Root and the Offspring of David, the Bright and Morning   Star."
17 And the Spirit and the bride say, "Come!" And let him who hears say, "Come!" And let him who thirsts

come. Whoever desires, let him take the water of life freely.

A Warning

18 For I testify to everyone who hears the words of the prophecy of this book: If anyone adds to these things, God will add to him the plagues that are written in this book; 19 and if anyone takes away from the words of the book of this prophecy, God shall take away his part from the Book of Life, from the holy city, and *from* the things which are written in this book.

I Am Coming Quickly

20 He who testifies to these things says, "Surely I am coming quickly."

Amen. Even so, come, Lord Jesus! 21 The grace of our Lord Jesus Christ *be* with you all. Amen.

Revelation Chapters 7, 21 & 22 enlighten us on the question of the kind of things that will be absent in Heaven. I have listed below some of the things that would be absent in Heaven:

1. There will be no more sea. (Revelation 21:1). In this scripture sea stands for nations of the world and rebellious nations. There will be no more broken ties, no more wars and scandals.
2. There will be no more death. (Revelation 21:4). There will be no more funeral services, tombstones and goodbyes.

3. There will be no more sorrow. (Revelation 21:4). In Heaven there will be uninterrupted joy and emotional tranquillity.
4. There will be no more crying. (Revelation 7:17 & Revelation 21:4).
5. There will be no more pain. (Revelation 21:4).
6. There will be no more sun or moon. (Revelation 7:16, Revelation 21:23 & Revelation 22:5).
7. There will be no more abominations. (Revelation21:27, Revelation 21:8 & Revelation 22:15).
8. There will be no more hunger, thirst or heat. Revelation 7:16. In its place there will be the tree of life and the beauty of the paradise of God.

<u># Chapter 8</u>

<u>God's plans for satan and his followers</u>
<u>Revelation 20</u>

Satan Bound 1000 Years

1 Then I saw an angel coming down from heaven, having the key to the bottomless pit and a great chain in his hand. 2 He laid hold of the dragon, that serpent of old, who is *the* Devil and Satan, and bound him for a thousand years; 3 and he cast him into the bottomless pit, and shut him up, and set a seal on him, so that he should deceive the nations no more till the thousand years were finished. But after these things he must be released for a little while.

The Saints Reign with Christ 1000 Years

4 And I saw thrones, and they sat on them, and judgment was committed to them. Then *I saw* the souls of those who had been beheaded for their witness to Jesus and for the word of God, who had not worshiped the beast or his image, and had not received *his* mark on their foreheads or on their hands. And they lived and reigned with Christ for a thousand years. 5 But the rest of the dead did not live again until the thousand years were finished. This *is* the first resurrection. 6 Blessed and holy *is* he who has part in the first resurrection. Over such the second death has no power, but they shall be priests of God and of Christ, and shall reign with Him a thousand years.

Satanic Rebellion Crushed

7 Now when the thousand years have expired, Satan will be released from his prison 8 and will go out to deceive the nations which are in the four corners of the earth, Gog and Magog, to gather them together to battle, whose number *is* as the sand of the sea. 9 They went up on the breadth of the earth and surrounded the camp of the saints and the beloved city. And fire came down from God out of heaven and devoured them. 10 The devil, who deceived them, was cast into the lake of fire and brimstone where the beast and the false prophet *are*. And they will be tormented day and night forever and ever.

The Great White Throne Judgment

11 Then I saw a great white throne and Him who sat on it, from whose face the earth and the heaven fled away. And there was found no place for them. 12 And I saw the dead, small and great, standing before God, and books were opened. And another book was opened, which is *the Book* of Life. And the dead were judged according to their works, by the things which were written in the books. 13 The sea gave up the dead who were in it, and Death and Hades delivered up the dead who were in them. And they were judged, each one according to his works. 14 Then Death and Hades were cast into the lake of fire. This is the second death. 15 And anyone not found written in the Book of Life was cast into the lake of fire.

1. Revelation 20:14-15 says that the lake of fire has been prepared by God for satan and his followers.
2. Revelation 20:10 also tells us that the place prepared by God for satan and his followers is a place of torment.

Characteristics of Hell

1. A place of torment. (Revelation 20:10)
2. A place of abandonment. (Luke 16:19-31, Isaiah 66:23-24 and Revelation 19:17-21).
3. A place of eternity (Revelation 20:10).
4. A place of easy access but no exits. Entering Hell is easy. All it takes is to be disobedient to God here on earth. (John 3:36).

<u>**Isaiah 66:23-24**</u>

23 And it shall come to pass
That from one New Moon to another,
And from one Sabbath to another,
All flesh shall come to worship
before Me," says the LORD.
24 " And they shall go forth and look
Upon the corpses of the men
Who have transgressed against Me.
For their worm does not die,
And their fire is not quenched.
They shall be an abhorrence to all flesh."

<u>Revelation 19:17-21</u>

The Beast and His Armies Defeated

17 Then I saw an angel standing in the sun; and he cried with a loud voice, saying to all the birds that fly in the midst of heaven, "Come and gather together for the supper of the great God, 18 that you may eat the flesh of kings, the flesh of captains, the flesh of mighty men, the flesh of horses and of those who sit on them, and the flesh of all *people,* free and slave, both small and great."

19 And I saw the beast, the kings of the earth, and their armies, gathered together to make war against Him who sat on the horse and against His army. 20 Then the beast was captured, and with him the false prophet who worked signs in his presence, by which he deceived those who received the mark of the beast and those who worshiped his image. These two were

cast alive into the lake of fire burning with brimstone. 21 And the rest were killed with the sword which proceeded from the mouth of Him who sat on the horse. And all the birds were filled with their flesh.

John 3:36

36 He who believes in the Son has everlasting life; and he who does not believe the Son shall not see life, but the wrath of God abides on him."

Chapter 9

Lessons we can learn from the way Jesus Christ died

1. Jesus Christ died with a mixture of grief and joy. Jesus knew that his death was the doorway leading back to his Father. At the same time he knew that his death was the path to victory for all those who believe in him. In Jesus' case although the exit was grievous the entrance into the presence of God was joyful. (Matthew 26:38, Matthew 26:42, John 17:5 & Hebrews 12:2).
2. Jesus died at the right time. (John 13:1, John 7:30 & John 8:20).
3. Jesus died in fulfilment of his purpose in life. He died on the

cross in order to save you and me and to reconcile us back to God.

4. Jesus died for the right purpose. He died within the will of God for his life. (John 17:11 & John 19:30).

5. Jesus died with the right attitude and commitment. (Luke 23:43 & Luke 23:46).

Chapter 10

How can we spend eternity with God in Heaven?

In order for us to have the privilege of spending eternity with God in Heaven, we need to note the following:

1. We must be citizens of Heaven. We need to have the passport marked with the shed blood of Jesus. A visa in another passport will not do.
2. We must also not imagine for a moment that we will get into Heaven without receiving Jesus Christ as Lord and saviour of our lives. We need to be born again in accordance with John 3:1-36.
3. In Heaven there will be no illegal immigrants. All those who will

end up in Heaven deserve to be in Heaven. God will not be making any mistakes about admissions. Only those who have a relationship with him through his son Jesus Christ will be granted entry into Heaven.

4. Going to Heaven is an individual matter. The choice is ours. The choice is only available to us today. As Jesus put it "… I have placed before you life and death. Choose life and live…"

5. Only those who have repented of their sins will be granted entry into Heaven. The Bible says in Proverbs 28:13 that "… he who covers his sins shall not prosper. But he who confesses and forsakes his sins shall obtain mercy…" Confession + Forsaking = Mercy (Repentance).

We therefore need to confess our sins and forsake our sins before we can gain entry into Heaven. The choice is ours.

6. No one can enter into Heaven without God's specific approval. The Bible says today is the day of salvation. My brother or sister, let us confess our sins and forsake them whilst we have the chance today. Tomorrow will be too late. As Jesus said "…let him who has ears to hear hear what the Lord is saying to the Church…" It is God's hearts desire that you and I not only be a part of the church community in word but also in deed.

7. To gain entry into Heaven, we need to believe in the finished work of Jesus Christ on the cross.

8. We need to receive Jesus into our hearts as our Lord and personal saviour.

9. We also need to receive the righteousness that God provides for us in Christ Jesus. (2 Corinthians 5:21, John 3:3, Romans 8:29-30, Romans 4:13 & Romans 8:38-39).

After we have received the free gift of salvation, God expects that we will begin to fulfil our call in life. If we begin to walk in our call, we will grow in it. When the time comes for us to die, we should be able to say "God is calling me and I must go" or "it is finished". The choice is ours.

We need to come to the point in our lives where we are able to say "…for me to live is Christ and to die is gain…" (Philippians 1:21-24, Hebrews 2:14-15 & 1Corinthians 15:55).

The Bible says in Revelation 14:13 that "… the dead in the Lord rest from their labours…" If you would like to have rest at the end of your labours here on earth then say this prayer with me:

Prayer:

Lord Jesus Christ,

I confess that I have sinned against you.

I thank you for dying on the cross for me and that you are alive today.

I come to you just as I am.

I want to know you in a real way.

Forgive my sins.

Change my life.

Show yourself to me and be my saviour and Lord everyday.

Amen.

Dear brother or sister, if you have said this prayer, I would like to welcome you into the Kingdom of God. The angels are rejoicing over your salvation as I am.

Conclusion

My brother or sister, one second after you die, what kind of welcome will await you? The choice is yours. It is my prayer that you will take the steps that will enable Jesus to welcome you into Heaven when you die.

Your death and my death are inevitable. We need to prepare for it. May the Lord help us to make the right choices on this side of life. See you in Heaven in Jesus' name – Amen.

If this book has blessed you in any way, we will like to hear your testimony. Simply write your testimony and send it to us.

Our Postal Address in the UK is: Wood World Missions

118-120 London Road

Mitcham, Surrey,

CR4 3LB

United Kingdom

E-mail Address: rev.dr.wood@hotmail.co.uk

Website: www.woodworldmissions.org

www.powercentre@chweb.org

International: +44 (208) 286 3018 UK Mobile: 07958 213 729

<u>**BIBLE SCHOOL**</u>**: Ring any of the above numbers for information about the Wood World Missions' free Bible School in the United Kingdom.**

<u>**Mitcham & Morden Branch:**</u> Power Centre Church, Lavender Children's Centre, London Road, Mitcham, CR4 3LA

Service Times: 10.30am – 1pm

<u>**Wood World Missions Monthly Conference**</u>: **Held on the second Saturday of each month: VENUE:** Lavender Children's Centre, London Road, Mitcham, CR4 3LA

Time: 6.30pm to 9.30pm – Refreshments Provided.

<u>**Please ring to confirm the venue of our meetings before attending. Thanks.**</u>

STAY BLESSED IN JESUS NAME

Copyright (c) 2007

Wood World Missions & Power Centre Church

(To the glory of God)

www.ingramcontent.com/pod-product-compliance
Lightning Source LLC
Chambersburg PA
CBHW022120050726
47591CB00002B/857